EDGE BOOKS

NASCAR RACING

NASCAR's Greatest Moments

by Matt Doeden

Consultant:
Suzanne Wise, Librarian
Stock Car Racing Collection, Belk Library
Appalachian State University
Boone, North Carolina

Capstone *press*

Mankato, Minnesota

Edge Books are published by Capstone Press,
151 Good Counsel Drive, P.O. Box 669, Mankato, Minnesota 56002.
www.capstonepress.com

Library of Congress Cataloging-in-Publication Data
Doeden, Matt.
    NASCAR's greatest moments / by Matt Doeden.
    p. cm.—(Edge books. NASCAR racing)
    Summary: "Describes some of the greatest moments in NASCAR history,
including photo finishes, wild wrecks, and intense rivalries between drivers"—Provided
by publisher.
    Includes bibliographical references and index.
    ISBN–13: 978-1-4296-0086-6 (hardcover)
    ISBN–10: 1-4296-0086-1 (hardcover)
    1. NASCAR (Association)—History—Juvenile literature. 2. Stock car racing—
United States—History—Juvenile literature. 3. Automobile racing drivers—United
States—Biography—Juvenile literature. I. Title.
GV1029.9.S74D637 2008
796.72—dc22   2007000252

Editorial Credits

Aaron Sautter, editor; Jason Knudson, set designer; Patrick D. Dentinger, book designer;
    Jo Miller, photo researcher

Photo Credits

AP/Wide World Photos, John Bazemore, 25; John Russell, 6; NASCAR, Hand Out, cover;
    Ric Feld, 18, 20; The Morning News, Alison Sidlo, 13; Wade Payne, 5
Corbis/Bettmann, 11, 17; GT Images/George Tiedemann, 22, 28
Getty Images Inc./Bill Hall, 26; Jamie Squire, 12
SportsChrome, Inc/Evan Pinkus, 9
The Sharpe Image/Sam Sharpe, 14

Cover photo: The closest finish in NASCAR history took place at the 2003
    Carolina Dodge Dealers 400 between Ricky Craven and Kurt Busch.

1 2 3 4 5 6 12 11 10 09 08 07

Table of Contents

Chapter 1
Signature Wins.................... 4

Chapter 2
Photo Finishes 10

Chapter 3
Playing Rough.................... 16

Chapter 4
The Bizarre 24

Down to the Last Lap 15

Junior's Biggest Win 23

NASCAR's Greatest Moments........ 29

Glossary 30

Read More 31

Internet Sites 31

Index 32

Signature Wins

Since 1947, NASCAR racing has grabbed the attention of fans across the United States. From wild wrecks to photo finishes, there's never a dull moment for race fans.

Intense rivalries between drivers have led to some of the sport's greatest moments. Most great NASCAR drivers have at least one big win over a rival that every fan remembers.

Gordon's Bump-and-Run

On August 24, 2002, the pressure to win at Bristol Motor Speedway was high for two NASCAR greats. Jeff Gordon hadn't won a race in 11 months. Rusty Wallace hadn't won in more than a year. Both drivers were hungry for victory lane.

Gordon dominated most of the Sharpie 500. But in the final laps, he found himself behind Wallace. With just three laps to go, Gordon saw his chance to take back the lead. When Wallace had to slow down in the turn, Gordon made his move.

Dale Earnhardt Jr. (#8), Jeff Gordon (#24), and Rusty Wallace (#2) led the pack at the start of the 2002 Sharpie 500.

Learn about:

→ The "bump-and-run"

→ Jeff Gordon's big win

→ Earnhardt's famous pass

5

The crowd roared as Gordon pulled up to Wallace's rear bumper. Although Gordon's car was faster, Wallace blocked the inside lane. Gordon knew he might not get another chance. He held his speed and gently tapped Wallace's rear bumper. The contact caused Wallace's rear tires to lift slightly. Without rear grip, the car slid to the high part of the track. As Wallace fought to regain control of his car, Gordon sped by on the inside.

Gordon celebrated his big win by doing a burn-out for the fans.

Wallace quickly recovered. He was mad and surely would have given Gordon's car the same treatment. But he never got the chance. Gordon roared across the finish line to the cheers and boos of the crowd. The famous "bump-and-run" move led Gordon back to victory lane. Meanwhile, Wallace was left steaming.

"At a short track, if you can get to the rear bumper and give him a little tap, it's going to happen. You expect it from them and they should expect it from you."
—Jeff Gordon, *Sports Illustrated.com*, 8-27-02

The "Pass in the Grass"

NASCAR's all-star race is a unique event. Drivers don't earn Cup points as they do in most races, but there's a huge payday for the winner. Drivers take big risks to win the big money. Their all-or-nothing strategy was evident at the 1987 event.

In the race's final 10 laps, Dale Earnhardt Sr. was up front with Geoffrey Bodine and Bill Elliott. Earnhardt was nicknamed "The Intimidator." He was never afraid to bump an opponent. When he bashed into Elliott's car, Elliott decided to hit back. He tapped Earnhardt from behind, causing Earnhardt's car to veer onto the grassy infield.

It looked like Earnhardt would spin out in the grass. But somehow, he kept his car under control. He mashed the accelerator and sped through the infield. When he moved back onto the track, he was ahead of Elliott and Bodine. His famous "Pass in the Grass" didn't just save him from a wreck, it also helped him win the race!

Dale Earnhardt Sr. was famous for his aggressive driving style.

CHAPTER 2

Photo Finishes

Sometimes race finishes are very close, and drivers win by less than a single car length. Once in awhile, a finish is so close that the fans can't tell who won. Finishes like these make for some of the sport's greatest moments.

One classic finish came at the very first Daytona 500 in 1959. On the race's last lap, Lee Petty and Johnny Beauchamp battled to take the lead. As they neared the finish line, they came up on Joe Weatherly's car. Weatherly was running a lap behind. The three cars crossed the finish line side-by-side. Weatherly was on the high side, Petty in the middle, and Beauchamp on the low side.

Nobody was sure who won. Some officials believed it was Beauchamp, so his team celebrated in the pits. Most of the fans left believing he had won. But three days later, NASCAR declared Petty the winner based on photographs of the finish. Now that was a real photo finish!

The first Daytona 500 had many exciting moments, including this spin-out of Fred McGuirk's #16 car.

Learn about:

➜ The first Daytona 500
➜ Ricky Craven's historic win
➜ The 2004 race for the Cup

Ricky Craven and Kurt Busch fought for the lead in the final turn of the 2003 Carolina Dodge Dealers 400.

A Historic Finish

The closest finish in NASCAR history came at Darlington Raceway on March 16, 2003. With 23 laps to go, Kurt Busch took the lead when Jeff Gordon was caught in a wreck. Busch held the lead for 20 laps, but Ricky Craven was inching closer on every lap. Finally, Craven caught Busch.

The two raced side-by-side with two laps to go. Craven nudged Busch to take a small lead. But Busch came right back, bumping Craven a little harder. Craven's car flew to the high side of the track, and Busch regained the lead.

Busch held that slim lead entering the final turn of the race. But as the cars came onto the final stretch, they were again side-by-side. Busch and Craven charged toward the checkered flag. Their cars bumped and ground together as they crossed the finish line. To the naked eye, it looked like a tie. The crowd roared, still unsure who had won.

Craven and Busch's cars locked together as they crossed the finish line.

Ricky Craven won the closest finish NASCAR has ever seen.

Finally, NASCAR's electronic scoring monitor settled the question. Craven had crossed the finish line just .002 seconds before Busch. He'd just won the closest race in NASCAR history.

"It's awesome. That's what it's all about—racing as hard as you can. I drove the Ford the best I could and came up a bit shy, I guess."

—Kurt Busch, *NASCAR.com*, 4-02-03

Down to the Last Lap

In 2004, Kurt Busch won one of the closest Cup championships in history. Entering the season's final race, he, Jeff Gordon, and Jimmie Johnson were all close in the standings. Busch led Johnson by only 18 points and Gordon by 21. Even a few positions could mean the difference between a championship and third place.

Johnson and Gordon finished second and third respectively. Busch did just enough by finishing fifth. He won the title by just 8 points over Johnson and 16 over Gordon. If Johnson had finished first instead of second, he would have taken the title.

CHAPTER 3

Playing Rough

A race doesn't have to be a photo finish to be exciting. Some of NASCAR's most memorable events have involved contact between cars. This was never truer than at the 1976 Daytona 500.

Late in the race, Richard Petty and David Pearson were battling for the lead. On the last lap, Pearson passed Petty on the high side. But Petty came roaring back, and the two entered the final turn side-by-side. As the cars came out of the turn, Petty's car slipped just a little bit. He bumped Pearson into the wall. Pearson bounced back into Petty, and both cars went spinning down the final frontstretch.

Petty's car spun into the grassy infield, sliding to a stop just a few feet short of the finish line. Meanwhile, Pearson's car spun toward the pits. He somehow managed to keep the car running and got it under control. The crowd went wild as Pearson's car crept over the finish line for the victory.

After the crash, Richard Petty's car was too damaged to finish the race.

Learn about:

→ A smashing finish in Daytona

→ Fighting on the backstretch

→ An accidental victory

Cale Yarborough (#11) lost control of his car and smashed into Donnie Allison (#1) at the 1979 Daytona 500.

Duking it out at Daytona

The 1979 Daytona 500 was one of the most important events in NASCAR's history. It was the first time an entire Cup race was broadcast live on national TV. When a snowstorm hit the East Coast, many people watched the race on TV at home. And they saw quite a show.

On the last lap, Donnie Allison held a small lead over Cale Yarborough. Richard Petty and Darrell Waltrip followed almost half a lap behind the leaders. On the backstretch, Yarborough tried to make a pass low. But Allison drove down to block him. Yarborough wouldn't give up, though. He drove even lower, until his tires tore into the muddy grass.

The car lurched and shot up the track, smashing into Allison. The cars locked together and crashed into the outside wall just before the final turn. Petty and Waltrip sped past, and Petty held on for the victory.

After the crash, Yarborough and Bobby Allison fought each other on the track.

Back at the crash, Yarborough, Allison, and Allison's brother Bobby got into a fight. The TV cameras captured it all. The drama of the race and the fight that followed played a big part in boosting NASCAR's popularity.

"The track was mine until he hit me in the back. He got me loose and sideways, so I came back to get what was mine. He wrecked me, I didn't wreck him."

—Donnie Allison, *No. 1: An Ending for the Ages,* DailyPress.com, 3-23-03

The Final Straightaway

In October 2006, NASCAR's Chase for the Nextel Cup was really heating up. Two of the contenders were Dale Earnhardt Jr. and Jimmie Johnson. After almost 500 miles (800 kilometers) of racing at Talladega Superspeedway, both drivers were in good shape to move up in the standings. Earnhardt was running in first, with Johnson close behind.

Johnson had one big advantage over Earnhardt. His teammate, Brian Vickers, was drafting right behind him. Johnson hoped that his teammate would help push him past Earnhardt on the final straightaway. With a draft from ahead and behind, Johnson dove low. Vickers' job was to follow him. But Vickers was nervous and made a mistake. He swerved down into Johnson's rear bumper. The contact caused Johnson to lose control of his car. Johnson slammed into Earnhardt's car, and both of them spun out of control.

Vickers, meanwhile, was unaffected by the contact. He sped by Johnson and Earnhardt to take the checkered flag. But Vickers' first career win wasn't quite how he'd imagined it. The fans booed him loudly. Worse still, his own teammates were furious with him.

Vickers (#25) drafted close behind Johnson (#48) in the 2006 UAW Ford 500.

Junior's Biggest Win

One of the most emotional wins in NASCAR history came at the Pepsi 400 in July 2001. Six months earlier, Dale Earnhardt Sr. was killed in a wreck at the Daytona 500. The Pepsi 400 was NASCAR's first race at Daytona International Speedway after his death. Earnhardt's son, Dale Jr., badly wanted to win to honor his father's memory.

Junior did exactly that. He dominated the race and used good pit strategy to stay out front most of the day. After taking the checkered flag, Dale Jr. did a big burnout in the infield grass as the crowd's cheers filled the air.

CHAPTER 4

The Bizarre

NASCAR is full of close finishes, wild wrecks, and thrilling passes. But some of the sport's most memorable moments are also the strangest.

The final race of the 1992 season was unusual in many ways. It was Jeff Gordon's first Cup race and Richard Petty's last. Plus, an amazing six drivers still had a chance to win the championship.

As the race wore on, only two drivers were left with a chance at the title. Bill Elliott ran in first place. Alan Kulwicki was second. Kulwicki had considered himself a big underdog to win the championship. He even removed the first two letters of the word "Thunderbird" on his car so that it read "Underbird" instead.

Richard Petty ended his final race with his car smashed and on fire.

Learn about:

→ The "Underbird"

→ Racing on truck tires

→ Great **NASCAR** moments

Elliott held on to win the race. But because Kulwicki had led for one more lap than Elliott, he got 5 bonus points. The bonus points were enough to lift Kulwicki over Elliott to win the championship. Kulwicki celebrated by driving a clockwise lap around the track. It was probably the most famous celebration in NASCAR history.

Kulwicki called his car the "Underbird" because he thought his chances to win the 1992 championship were small.

He Did What?

No NASCAR race could be stranger than the 1950 Southern 500 at Darlington Raceway. It was NASCAR's first race at Darlington, and a whopping 75 cars started the race. Many of the entrants had driven their race cars across the country to get to the track.

The newly paved surface at the track was rough. Tires wore out constantly. Every car but one made frequent pit stops. That one car belonged to Johnny Mantz. Mantz had guessed correctly that tough truck tires would handle Darlington's racing surface better than car tires. He drove his Plymouth at a slow speed near the infield on a low, narrow part of the track called the apron. With everyone else constantly changing their tires in the pits, Mantz won by nine laps. The race took almost seven hours, and his average winning speed was just 75 miles (120 kilometers) per hour.

NASCAR has come a long way since the early days. But it still has its share of thrilling moments and dramatic finishes. Wild wrecks and photo finishes can happen at any time. Fans love NASCAR racing because they never know when they might get to see the sport's next great moment.

Fans love the thrill and excitement of NASCAR racing. They never know what might happen on the track.

NASCAR'S
Greatest Moments

1950—Johnny Mantz uses truck tires and takes it slow on the apron to beat out 74 other drivers at the first Southern 500.

1959—In the first Daytona 500, Lee Petty beats Johnny Beauchamp in a photo finish.

1970—Buddy Baker sets a closed course speed record of 200 miles (322 kilometers) per hour.

1976—David Pearson and Richard Petty collide and spin out in the final frontstretch; Pearson slowly rolls across the finish line to win.

1980—Dale Earnhardt Sr. wins the first of seven Cup championships.

1992—Richard Petty drives in his final Cup race; newcomer Jeff Gordon drives in his first. In the same race, Alan Kulwicki wins one of the closest Cup championships in history.

1998—After 19 years of bad luck, racing legend Dale Earnhardt Sr. finally wins his first Daytona 500.

2004—Kurt Busch wins the Chase for the Cup by just 8 points over Jimmie Johnson.

2006—Jimmie Johnson overcomes a huge deficit in the standings to win his first Cup championship.

Glossary

apron (AY-pruhn)—the narrow strip of pavement that separates the infield of some tracks from the racing surface

backstretch (BAK-strech)—the long, straight part of a racetrack that sits opposite the finish line

frontstretch (FRUHNT-strech)—the long, straight part of a racetrack that contains the finish line

infield (IN-feeld)—the enclosed area in the center of a racetrack where race teams are located during a race

pits (PITZ)—the area on a racetrack where cars go to get service from a pit crew; the pits are usually just inside the frontstretch.

straightaway (STRAYT-uh-way)—a long, straight part of a racetrack between turns; cars reach their highest speeds on the straightaways.

underdog (UHN-der-dawg)—a person or team that is not expected to win an event

Read More

Eagen, Rachel. *NASCAR*. Automania! New York: Crabtree, 2006.

Johnstone, Michael. *NASCAR*. The Need for Speed. Minneapolis: LernerSports, 2002.

Schaefer, A. R. *The History of NASCAR*. NASCAR Racing. Mankato, Minn.: Capstone Press, 2005.

Internet Sites

FactHound offers a safe, fun way to find Internet sites related to this book. All of the sites on FactHound have been researched by our staff.

Here's how:
1. Visit *www.facthound.com*
2. Choose your grade level.
3. Type in this book ID code **1429600861** for age-appropriate sites. You may also browse subjects by clicking on letters, or by clicking on pictures and words.
4. Click on the **Fetch It** button.

FactHound will fetch the best sites for you!

Index

Allison, Bobby, 20
Allison, Donnie, 18, 19–20

Beauchamp, Johnny, 10, 29
Bristol Motor Speedway, 4
Busch, Kurt, 12–14, 15, 29

Carolina Dodge Dealers 400,
    12–14
championships, 15, 24,
    26, 29
Craven, Ricky, 12–14

Darlington Raceway, 12, 27
Daytona 500, 10, 11, 16,
    19–20, 23, 29
Daytona International
    Speedway, 23

Earnhardt Jr., Dale, 5,
    21–22, 23
Earnhardt Sr., Dale, 8, 9,
    23, 29
Elliott, Bill, 8, 24, 26

Gordon, Jeff, 4–7, 12, 15,
    24, 29

Johnson, Jimmie, 15,
    21–22, 29

Kulwicki, Alan, 24, 26, 29

Mantz, Johnny, 27, 29

"Pass in the Grass", 8
Pearson, David, 16, 29
Pepsi 400, 23
Petty, Lee, 10, 29
Petty, Richard, 16, 17, 19, 24,
    25, 29
photo finishes, 4, 10, 13–14,
    16, 24, 28

Sharpie 500, 4–7
Southern 500, 27, 29

Talladega Superspeedway, 21

UAW Ford 500, 22
"Underbird", 24, 26

Vickers, Brian, 21–22

Wallace, Rusty, 4–7
Waltrip, Darrell, 19
wrecks, 4, 8, 12, 16, 17, 18,
    19, 21, 24, 25, 28

Yarborough, Cale, 18, 19–20